NIGHT SCHOOL

NIGHT SCHOOL

MICHAEL STEVEN

OTAGO UNIVERSITY PRESS
Te Whare Tā o Te Wānanga o Ōtākou

for Schaeffer Lemalu
(1983–2021)

CONTENTS

THE GOLD PLAINS

INTERCITY BUS ELEGIES

'I'm not on your map. I'm a mystery.'
—*El-P*

DROPPED PIN: SYMONDS STREET, AUCKLAND

We were waiting for the song to finish
before we said our goodbyes again.
It was a number by the Foo Fighters
and we were gagging at how Dave Grohl
should've never become a guitarist
and front man, but stuck instead
to playing the muffled, lead-booted
breaks Nirvana made him famous for—
breaks he ganked from John Bonham.
By chance we were buying cigarettes
in the same store, at the same time.
From the top of Newton Gully
thirty years had passed since we got pinched
boosting Trumpets at the corner dairy
and Rodney first vanished from my life
when his parents sent him to board
at some posh school, just out of Cambridge.
Twenty years had passed since
we last drank at the Wakefield Hotel
and Rodney told me he was going
to be a star, or sell meth and die trying.

*

The song ended and the ads started
and Rodney began to get restless
when he told me the crew he was rolling with
collected debts from property developers
and worked private security details.
But in every one of Rodney's stories
there always lurked a dark subtext
that made his plans seem implausible
or else destined to end in failure,
like the time he got sent away for
importing *bodybuilding supplements*;
or the raves he promoted that never happened.
When I closed the door to his ride
Rodney vanished from my life again.
He was staring into the setting sun
like a rabbit caught in the headlights' beam,
or someone who is witness to their end
through a haze of weed smoke and Fahrenheit,
with the ad reader's velveteen voice
saying, 'When you get stuck in a hole
the first thing you gotta do is stop digging.'

THE PICTURE OF DOCTOR FREUD

DROPPED PIN: PIGEON MOUNTAIN, PAKURANGA, EAST AUCKLAND

Where the young boys of our area first practised
inherited strategies of defence and attack,
on misted-out, wet Saturday mornings.
We wore boots tarred with Nugget polish.
Orange and green jumpers, the club colours.
Hungover fathers in nylon windbreakers
stood and scrutinised the state of play,
huffing obstinate cigarettes on the sideline.

I remember when one half of the mountain,
the side where the pā once faced the ocean,
fell down and they made the BMX track.
Before Fletchers grew a subdivision here,
you could pick buckets of wild mushrooms.
My father browned them off in butter and garlic.

THE PICTURE OF DOCTOR FREUD

Pinned to the wall above his office desk
my father's picture of Doctor Freud
was part of a salon hang: business cards,

invoices, pink dockets and packing slips,
photos of Ford Falcon GT 351s,
his framed, sun-faded Trade Certificate.

My father was no reader of psychoanalysis,
but of human nature he knew a lot.
He kept us fed in a world of sharks

while suited pig-hunter economists
filleted the country with Bowie knives.
Outside the office a hand-painted sign

in bold red and black cursive script
stated his terms: *Cash Only. No Exceptions.*

*

It did not hang there out of reverence
for the thinker's dynamic theories,
my father's picture of Doctor Freud.

He did not know about Oedipus
or troubles of the unconscious.
His only business was before him.

Daily the wrecks would pile up
in my father's dusty panel shop.
Inside the spray booth: misting cars

with lead paint, distant as an astronaut.
Alone at his dark wood typist's desk:
my father filling quotes, invoices;

making calls to his illicit affairs,
under the picture of Doctor Freud.

*

The one time my grandfather visited
my father's work, he sat himself
beneath the picture of Doctor Freud.

His infidelities shipwrecked my grandmother
in a one-room Royal Oak bedsitter—
jacked her out on Valium, talkback radio.

He leant back casually in the guest's chair
to tell my father about his new wife.
Cigarette smoke curled in the air:

unstable, hostile and pyrophoric.
A river of bad blood, thirty years long,
running between them on that afternoon.

My father and grandfather, the same
wounded human: complicit, bewildered.

*

It would take years of staring at my father's
crude ink drawing of Doctor Freud
before I unlocked its ulterior meaning.

Here was the thinker's sallow profile
rendered female by formless Rorschach.
On the forehead of the great thinker,

the place where I found my entry point,
some small skin tag rose as a breast.
Where the left lens of his glasses rested,

his nose curved into her naked thigh.
The shadow of his eyebrow became her sex.
How many office walls, lunchrooms

and toilet stalls across the district of Penrose
held that gray-scaled image in facsimile?

*

High summer, 1991. In January's
unequivocal heat my father's picture
of Doctor Freud gave up its meaning.

Coalition planes and frigates cindered
Iraq across our diurnal TV screens.
In a Salvation Army hospice

south of Maraetai, my grandfather
clocked out at sixty from a calcified liver.
At the local school I killed boredom.

I came here every weekend to suck
down purloined cigarettes, syrupy port.
Viridescent flaxes edged the fields,

the drab clusters of prefab classrooms,
and the neighbours' yards brochure-neat.

*

Through a knot-shaped hole in a fence paling
Jim Fisher's older sister dropped her robe
to the sun. I watched her nakedness

bending to meet the bright midday light.
I saw the ovoid birthmark on her ribcage
burning redder than Jupiter's storm.

I saw the secret delta, dark with hair.
The days of that summer become one day.
A day when desire's untenable music

seemed distant, esoteric: more complex
than algebra. And the inscription scrawled
across my father's crude ink drawing

of Doctor Freud, would read something
other than simply *What's on a Man's Mind.*

DROPPED PIN: MARAMARUA, EAST WAIKATO

Lessons. In the house that once stood,
where bricks and clumps of yarrow
wend and weave the space of extinction,
mornings came thick with blanket fog,
the tang of diesel, the spice of pipe tobacco.
Penned calves waited to die at the gate.
Trucks keened eastward along State Highway 2,
stopping at farms, inland towns, abattoirs.
Lessons. In a year I can never get back
I was sent here to change my behaviour.
I learnt instead the reprieve of a desk in a room.
My uncle gave me booze, word music.
He kept leatherbound volumes of verse
in a low cabinet beside his Johnny Walker.

DROPPED PIN: EASTERN BEACH, EAST AUCKLAND

Mr Jenkins had never been a student of Oxford.
Over his starched white business shirts
and cheap red polyester neckties
he sported the college's monogrammed jumper.
The mind of an old disciplinarian ruled
the body of a man-boy, fresh from his years
at teacher's college. Every time he shouted
to order our class of attention-deficit
hyperactive little shits, his voice
fractured like a glass reed
in crescendo.

            The best seat was by the window.
Bogans roared past school in their clapped-out
Holden Toranas and Mk.IV Cortinas.
Pastie would be rolling tinnies at his kitchen table,
waiting for the rush of after-school custies.
Tradies would put down their power tools and aprons
to pause under the sun's platinum rays.
My world entire might have started
and ended in the spume floating on the shoreline.
There was no malice or anger in his gaze
when Jenkins slammed his fist down on my desk.
He did not put me on after-school detention,
or shout at me to leave his classroom.

                        No—

he looked me in the eyes and passed a typed
copy of some poem called Thunder Road
and said, 'Here. This 'll teach you what I can't.'

STRAINS: WHITE WIDOW

—for Shantibaba

Back then, this is what I knew about Amsterdam.
It was a city in a landlocked European country
famous for Rembrandt's *Nightwatch*,

the Heineken Brewery, canals and tulips.
Steve had made it something of a spiritual home.
His version of Mecca was cobbled together

from stories told to him by travellers
of the mythical doper cafés in its red-light district,
articles he'd read in *High Times* magazine—

he would go there when the boss signed off his hours.
Until then, it was a smoko shed pipe dream.
Auckland grew fat on the milk of offshore money.

We were apprentice sparkies farmed out as crews
of cheap labour across the city by capitalist
bastards making bank on Freemason memberships.

Steve copped the zip off a patched biker at lunchtime.
It cost us each a week's wages. We said goodbye
to our co-workers, off for their Friday piss-up

and amphetamine session at the Queen's Ferry.
We stayed back. Burnt zoots in the site basement.
Two puffs in, my heart was working harder.

There was time dilation, cognitive dissonance.
Then came a sense of the weighty
and impractical burden of movement, speech.

Steve nosed the van out of the Bledisloe Building carpark
into the peak flow of Friday afternoon traffic,
laughed at me throwing a whitey beside him

in the passenger seat and said, 'You can say goodbye
to ditch weed that looks and tastes like bark.
Say goodbye to caps of runny green oil from Northland.

The weed of the future is grown hydroponically,
with high-EC nutrient systems and fast-flowering genetics
from the seed collections of plant wizard stoners.'

I'm thankful my life was altered and saved back then
by Johnny Appleseeds like my ol' mucker Steve,
and the talents of an Aussie breeder living in Amsterdam.

PAPA JACKS

Ballers in black merino with Thracian topknots
guarded the door to this hallowed dive bar,
enforcing their arcane entry code.
It seemed to change from week to week.
Before MMA, they were tournament kickboxers
moonlighting as gangland debt collectors.
Their reps kept the order in Vulcan Lane.
Grunge was the big thing and every plumber
with Pearl Jam's *Ten* on cassette rocked
checked flannels, Doc boots, frayed denim shorts
and grew their hair long like Mikey Havoc.
They came here to drink, pick up arts students.
Idiots on acid used to jump off the balcony.
Seattle was another suburb in Central Auckland.

WHEEL UP: 1997

In the dancehall of deep memory
it will always be four o'clock
on a Friday morning.

An MC is there up the front
shelling syncopated bars,
hyping a sea of pilled-out ravers

graffiti writers, till poppers,
backroom lurkers,
spliff builders

and shard roasters
screaming for the rewind
beneath the smoke

and strobing lasers
in a long-gone club
called Herzog.

WINTER CONDITIONS

TWO WOLVES

Wisdom arrives in the least expected of places.
Like the windowless basement bedroom
in a boarding house off Newton Gully,
rented by a speed-blasting tow-truck driver.
It was the season of yellow biker sulphate—
speed that sang in your throat like a spinning top
moments after you'd got your shot away.
Meth was a year off. This was the best ever.
We'd just scored off a hooker on the second floor.
The bro was cooking up by candlelight.
Lamps were blown or missing in every socket.
His grease-black hands and gnarled fingers
trembled as he aimed the dart into a broken vein.
And when the drug settled on his heart's ventricles,
its event horizon: the white flash of inspiration.
He chewed his gums and began a sermon,
'Every person has two wolves inside of them:
the good wolf and the evil wolf.' The gear
was wet and smelled like a hot pool
and the bro started cooking up his next shot.
'How we survive depends on which wolf we feed.'
When my bro winced before the candle's light,
I could see his two wolves were eating each other.

WINTER CONDITIONS

Autumn was ending. The new season's hard winds
blew sad phrases across our sidereal city.
The yellow harbour lights, no longer familiar,

spelt out their distance to me in cold semaphore.
Horns clanged on docking container ships,
arriving from the ports we would never visit.

Too many powder portents taken out of context.
Hours before, I confronted the silhouette
of your lover undressing by the bedroom door.

Ebb of the blood tide running through our days.
Love dwindled below us to metaphor.
Crossing over the bridge was pure nausea.

*

Unhinged, deranged. So insular and retracted,
my body soon merged with the car. Pistons
screamed in the soft housing of my stomach.

Gelid air blasted through the front windows.
My lungs opened. The carburettor throttled.
Every gearshift accelerated a rage suppressed.

I was the car, the car passing the pump houses
and humming turbines of the water treatment plant,
the shrinking factories and star-shaped suburbs.

Petrol tankers and late-night speeding couriers
hugged the inside lanes. Neil Young wailed
ragged loneliness through the Alpine speakers.

*

After the dark, vertiginous lanes of the motorway
came the satellite districts' hazy amber lights.
Moon-bright, Colonel Sanders' cackling skull

topped a stanchion pole on Ōrewa's main street.
Boy racers sipped beers outside the surf club,
slouching on the bonnets of their tinted sedans,

as if we happened upon them, there in the carpark,
conducting some kind of seismic experiment—
subwoofer boxes in open boots bumped anthemic

jump tunes by The Prodigy and Chemical Brothers.
Bass quakes rattled the shopfront windows.
The local copper rolled past their gathering twice.

*

Most of our friends indentured themselves
to student loans and generic educations.
Some would find God and never move away,

while others who had once been altar boys
put on ski-masks and preached with shotguns
to suburban bank-tellers, elderly pharmacists.

Most would blindly follow an inherited model:
careers, mortgages, the trappings of respectability.
That wasn't for me. I could never roll like that.

What I sought was a kind of psychic repatriation,
some way of harmonising with the ineffable.
Nihilism was chic in the decade we came up in.

*

We kept up our silence. Unhinged, deranged.
At this late hour, how could we be other,
when in the basement clubs and warehouses

the lean ablations of the chemical season
before this new century had already done us over.
The clocks did not stop as they had predicted.

I had wanted to leave it all behind us in the city,
the margins of blame, the games of attrition,
our new lovers waiting in their rented bedrooms.

Roused to action by the breakers' calm cadences,
your hand trembled into place on my thigh.
Our last rite. A new season. Autumn was ending.

DROPPED PIN: KINGSLAND, AUCKLAND

Like spending our days and nights in a suit of fire.
What other way did we have to explain it,
our secret? In summertime, while our friends
bared and bathed their bodies on Auckland beaches,
we suffered in the fug of darkened bedrooms.

Beneath our clothes were bodies mapped out
with lesions that wept like the Euphrates.
Nerves hewn raw by the song of hydrocortisone:
we self-prescribed our replacement therapies.

You were orphaned in a ruined country where children
make rhymes about airstrikes and bomb blasts,
but I choose to think of you holding court
in a bar of bikers, fauxhemians, pseudo-intellectuals.

Or the night we were tripping on magic mushrooms
while your boyfriend practised fader scratches
over the instrumental of Dr Doom's 'Apartment 223'.
That clandestine kiss you blew across the lounge
blasted the fourth wall. It fucked with time and space.

CHARLES SPEAR AT NEW BRIGHTON

M had given up drugs and working in parlours.
She was in the final year of a degree
training to be a social worker
when I met her. Every Saturday

she volunteered at the clinic on Gloucester Street,
driving a carload of detoxing addicts
in her Toyota hatchback
out to walk the pier at New Brighton.

The city was swatched in shades of immutable grey—
leeched of colour like a Hammershøi scene.
We were sitting alone in her car
watching the squalls and ladders of rain.

She let me smoke with the window down,
and gave me a dog-eared paperback
of Curnow's *Anthology of New Zealand Verse*.
It was June. My first winter in the South Island.

*

She was setting down her theory about why a city
with so many churches was also a catchment
pool for prisoners and psychiatric patients,
and how the city still operated

an unlegislated Brahminic class system,
when he rapped his knuckles against the driver's window.
He was wearing a creased gabardine coat
and looked vacant or confused.

He spoke like a man with a mouthful of ashes.
He told us he dreamt of a lost Europe,
then muttered the soft-syllabled lines
to which his reputation is given,

the indifferent rain falling through his hands and face
as if he was now no more than his poems,
no more than an interference of light
on a Saturday afternoon in New Brighton.

DROPPED PIN: HĀWERA, SOUTH TARANAKI

A road trip, years ago. The square
of acid my mate and I split
kicked in about here.

I'd wanted to show him the cheap
memorial plaque to Aotearoa's
greatest outlaw novelist.

A provincial jazz freak with an ear
for the brassy thump of ragtime,
for the laconically

menacing speech patterns
of grousing cockies and slaughterers
conspiring at high tables,

oiling their aggression
with whiskey and ale chasers.

*

Hungry shark plying his hustle daily
in louche basement pool halls.
Troubled by leggy harlots,

yoked to his widowed mother.
A cohort of bookies in bad suits
scheming in phone boxes,

scrap dealers and bent publicans.
He worked the blind family doctor
for amphetamine scripts.

Nicotine stains to his forearms,
he slapped and plucked
the strings of a double bass

in boozy barnyard dances
each weekend across the district.

*

We'd just smoked a joint of Northern Lights #5.
Inanimate objects began sending signals.
The trigger was a smirking Furby

swinging from a car's rearview mirror.
I remember gassing with laughter
at how the drive-thru

was rammed with hungover
farmers in flat-deck Hiluxes,
spotty-faced boy racers

and hardcore motherfuckers
with haircuts like Mad Max extras
rolling in battered Holdens.

To the right of the KFC counter:
the cheap gold plaque for Ron Morrieson.

ANIMAL KINGDOM

Blood from some morning blue between inmates
pooled on the steel floor of the prison truck.
It was Canterbury's coldest winter in fifteen years.
Ten of us shivered on benches in the back.
An old timer who had been sent down for a big one
studied the facial expressions and mannerisms
of a nervous, recidivist drunk-driver—
he'd be the first to lose his shoes and dinner.
Christchurch Prison was a long hour's drive from court.
The heater was broken. A car thief chased
meth off a crumpled piece of tinfoil.
I looked at the bloodstain, sliding like a film
of viscous red oil across a plane of frozen water.
The old timer unpicked the cuff of his denim jacket
for matches and a racehorse of Port Royal.
He lit it up, took a few puffs, and handed it on.
There wasn't much left by the time it came to me.
It was still nicotine. I puffed on it gratefully,
ducking under the guards' observation window.
'Relax, mate,' the old timer sniggered,
'You can't get sent to prison twice in one day.'

A METHODIST FAMILY PORTRAIT

The patriarch is, of course, centre of the photograph,
        surrounded by his four-son progeny.

Hard hands clasping the crook of a walking cane,
      this man who meted out discipline

in the name of the father, the son, the holy ghost:
      terror begins in his stare.

To his right, his youngest son: Hector, my great-grandfather.
      A boy in a world of men, the youngest

by seven years, he wears woollen shorts and knee-length,
      charcoal walk socks,

and a dark three-button over-shirt.
      As if following an order, his hands are fixed at his sides.

*

Hector's eyes give it all away: the pathological terror,
    the deep ancestral dread.

    The same terror and dread I would learn
in my father's eyes some evenings after he'd been drinking,

    as if he had witnessed his death,
and carried inside him the knowledge of life's last spectacle,

    the details, everything except the hour
and day the spectacle would play out.

    Years ago, after spending the night
awake on amphetamines, I saw upon my face the same terror

    ringing out across time
in those rooms of early morning mirrors.

DRANSFIELD IN DARLINGHURST

Dusk. Forests burn at the city's edges.
In his garret room, the young poet starts over.
Silence will not pay the electricity bill,
the Jurassic landlord's back rent
or what's owed on tick to the dealer.

*

Day and night he feeds the poem parasite.
For this young poet, dreaming the impossible
road back home to Courland Penders,
the junctures of art, love, sex and poetry:
everything passes through the eye of a needle.

LINES FOR JOE BOLTON

Nostalgia is a drug best dosed alone.
Like a bed holding the lovers' shapes
long after their tryst has ended
you wanted everything to remain,
in lines tender as the Southern drawl.
Poetry: your personal grief lexicon.

*

Florida nights, their punitive humidity.
Desire schooled you its crueler lessons.
From the window of some fleabag motel
you studied the neon's lingering trace.
You watched rain return as steam,
rising like a hymn off the hot bitumen.

COURBET IN PONSONBY

—for Garth Steeper

Divas in black lycra with dollar-dealing boyfriends
implore him to drink, to anger.

Their talk is boastful—
empty, irrelevant.

For the great realist painter
leaning against

the bar's cool
wooden

surface,
drinking

his eighteenth
nightly beer

there can only be one enduring language.
Beneath his skin, love moves

like a tapeworm.
God's pure language:

the carnal
body.

TROUBADOURS

—for Justin Townes Earle

In a nameless tavern where the beer is warm
and comes only in bottles, the barkeep
buffs the counter top with his red bandanna.

That drinker with his head turned down
is arranging peanut skins and bottle caps
into a diorama of desert sorrow.

America kills then builds its sad constellations
one star at a time: giving them names
like Williams, Van Zandt, Molina.

Unusable quarters jam the silent jukebox.
Across the carpark, the lights come on
at the Motel Six. In rooms you rent

by the hour, another of Walt Whitman's children
collect-calls his dealer. Quarters are unusable.
The jukebox is muted in these parts.

Death glides on highways in a black Lincoln.

STRAINS: NORDLE

—for Howard Marks

One by one his team turned against him.
Made to snitch by DEA strongarming
handlers with nefarious agendas
for lesser sentences, new identities
in the pre-fab life of witness protection.
He held his silence. He took the years.
He taught literacy to mafia capos,
biker bosses, top shotta Dominicans.
Meanwhile, the hustle of money and arms
set fire to the Mazar's hash fields.
First it was the Russians; then the steam-
rolling forces of the US military—
opium became the big money crop.
Back home in Majorca, hashish has gone.
Grown by illegal Vietnamese immigrants,
the weed they burn is full of chemicals—
weed that has lost its magic and wonder.
The aging smuggler has one last call to make.
Every weed nerd in the world knows
his codeword to enter history was 'Nordle'.

STRAINS: DURBAN POISON

—for Peter Madden

Long before an unsigned rapper named Berner
and his team from the Bay Area chucked
F1 Durban pollen on a female pheno of OG Kush

creating the hype-chaser's dream known as GSC
(or Girl Scout Cookies, as it used to be called),
this sativa strain was well on its way to infamy.

It is the strain grown by the protagonist's daughter
in J.M. Coetzee's eighth novel, *Disgrace*.
Back in the 70s, Otago poet John Dickson

smoked some that had come off a phosphate ship—
spring-boarding the gnosis of his psychonautic
odyssey, 'The Four Sided Square and Other Mysteries'.

My flatmate and I once bought fifty bucks' worth
off a stranger at the Beachhaven Mobil, in '97.
It was moss-coloured and stunk of sweet Lemon Pledge.

DROPPED PIN: ALAPPUZHA, SOUTH INDIA

Alimony is not a word they use around here
but it's what Bob Dylan sings for tonight
through the rooftop casino's speaker-box.
Tables of gamblers smoke counterfeit Marlboros,
play hands of 500 for stacks of grimy rupees.

They look out along the Laccadive shoreline,
where groups of effigies burn until dawn.
God is a ghost here with three tongues—
juggernauts sing him through dusty streets.
Smoke eats the sea. He first got here in 100 AD.

THE GOLD PLAINS

STRAINS: EXODUS CHEESE

Across the towns of England and Scotland:
Thatcher's face on a thousand pub dartboards.
People were broke and so they came together
and danced and danced, off their chops
on MDMA that was cheap and free of eutylone—
one big fuck you to the government and cops.
Ravers in the place of Luton got their skank on
in farmers' paddocks and warehouse squats.
Techno anarchists, dropouts and ferals,
the weed they grew kept the dance running.
Breakbeat culture was built with drum machines,
samplers and synthesisers, silver Rizlas,
and this odorous phenotype of Skunk #1
found in a ten-pack of beans from Sensi Seeds.

DROPPED PIN: TRINITY WHARF, TAURANGA

They can feel it coming on along the esplanade.
Itinerant backpackers from Belgium,
Cork and Essex, parked up by the inlet

burning a little weed and tobacco:
attuned to the drillings of oystercatchers,
the drone of dragonfly flight paths.

Bass-freaks in their supercharged Holdens
bumping DMX's gruff battle verses
slow to an idle for judder bars.

Even the hard-arse biker riding a gold hog
de-clutches, drops his scowl,
coasting past the cafés and pubs.

Retired sports hosts, aging rock stars,
shift their wax wives into the shade.

*

Gulls bum-rush weekenders outside the fishery.
Swoop oily paper parcels of chips, tarikihi.
Two workers on break, bloodied boots and aprons,

disappear behind gusts of grape vape cloud.
Kahawai, gutted snapper and ling stare
back at customers from crushed-ice beds.

The young cook jostling baskets of orders
across banks of spitting tallow fryers
wipes the late-afternoon torpor off her face

with her apron's edge, her red-starred forearm.
On coastlines and farms, in towns and cities,
death is wholesaled to human appetite.

Next to sauce bottles stacked neatly in rows
the radio belts out another auto-tuned summer.

*

The old lady peeling potatoes in a white bucket
by the back door, tilts her face upwards.
She knows it too. It's spelling itself

to the girls waving down at us from a wall
of flowering orange nasturtium.
It's right there, in the haze descending

on the bridge's six sweeping lanes,
in the low thrum of semis hauling trailers,
double-cab utes pulling hobby boats

out to the serpentine suburbs.
The beach beyond, that blue arc of water,
is the city's perpetual rhythm track.

A white noise generator intoning
its hothouse days, its noir-score nights.

*

My friend tells me bad things happen here.
Once, he said, a man was made to kneel
under the town side of the bridge,

where the band play prog rock covers
through stacks of Peavey speakers,
and forced to kiss the end of a shotgun.

They clipped him, collected the bounty.
Slipped back out through Customs
on newly minted counterfeit passports.

The powerful build seaside palaces.
Make window offerings to the sun.
Money seeps through porous borders:

regular as clockwork, ectothermic.
The edge of heaven is an infinity pool.

*

Another city, the city he left behind for this one.
My father threads the black steering wheel
of a dead man's ride through his gnarled hands.

His new wife, shocked silent behind her dark glasses,
watches avenues of villas and bungalows
waking to blueness. It is a Sunday,

our last meal, the car ghosting to memory.
They call him a coward, her dead ex-husband.
They blame his death on sleeping pills,

on the grey plastic bag he wore as a hood.
They broke his heart. It killed his will to live.
Today alcohol made me leave the table

and walk towards a man I mistook for my father.
Forgive me: our silence stretches a decade.

*

Forever is an orgasm in this floating hotel.
Our rented kingdom of white towelling,
crumpled sheets, cheap wine riffs,

movies we'd make rather than watch.
It does not matter that behind the curtains
there is only an empty parking lot

and a sad red overflowing dumpster.
In the light that wakes us to want again,
all I want right now are your thighs

parting before me like cathedral doors,
your name's two-syllabled psalm
ringing from my tongue tip in rapture.

All I want is to lose myself right now
in your heat, the wet heat of this forever.

*

Should I tell you about my first visit here?
1995. My youth ended that summer.
Weekdays, I grubbed it. A sparky's apprentice.

Took lessons after work from psychonauts.
In a state house on Pilkington Road
we scored trips, bullets of Afghan indica.

We read Kerouac, Camus and Blake.
Memorised the esoteric ghetto parables
of the GZA's solo album, *Liquid Swords*.

We wanted all we could of a world
beyond the streets of our dim suburb.
Here I wept on acid for my fractured family.

Unable to name the mind I was losing,
I was alone in a realm outside of language.

*

My dream ends with the aircon's cool drone.
Blue pilot light roaming the dark room.
Your metricated breaths rise and fall

beside me on the bed, soft and familiar.
Drunken tourists argue out in the corridor.
I can't decipher what they are saying,

or what makes them argue so publicly,
so fiercely. Only their muffled rage
passes through the tilt-slab concrete walls.

Sleep clocks the hours until check out.
The receptionist on graveyard shift
will be scrolling her favourite newsfeeds.

Deep beneath the marbled foyer
molten clefts of magma lurch together.

DROPPED PIN: ADDINGTON, CHRISTCHURCH

—for Jordan Hamel

My one honest job while living in Christchurch
was working night shift at the PDL factory,
on the outskirts of Addington.
We sat like monkeys in a windowless room
for nine hours straight: collared with earth strap
bonds to metal workbenches,
soldering weevil-shaped resistors
and capacitors to printed circuit boards.
The three of us sat at the same bench.
Rona came in each night from Hornby,
her breath gassy with bad port.
Dave with his spade beard,
snarling, 'Whoever masters the weather
is the master of our emotions.'
I was grateful for any gig I could get.
The three of us sitting together—
our sponges and soldering irons,
our thimbles of flux and conspiracy theories.

*

We killed time with the same bad jokes,
the same sad *Classic Hits* playlist.
I scribbled secret lines of unspeakable
poetry inside notebooks, eager
for the buzzer to sound the shift's ending,
for the cool air to freshen my lungs
when I stepped into the night.
Five decades earlier my paternal grandfather
moved his young family north
to flee his tranquiliser addiction
and the blood-beat of Wesleyan hymns.
The only sermons I needed to hear
came through my headphones,
crossing the avenues and districts
of sirens and empty churches
of this dark city, back to my bedsitter
and hungry poem in my typewriter
waiting impatiently to be fed the next line.

DROPPED PIN: HIGH STREET, CENTRAL AUCKLAND

—for Dominic Hoey

Thursday night in the main room of The Box:
Manuel Bundy, Sirvere and Sub-Zero
chopped beats from record boxes and red crates.
The backpacker movement was in full swing.
Vinyl junkies mainlined their week's dole
or the money they made selling hydro
on the stylus at Truetone, then Beat Merchants.
I wrote screeds and screeds of unsayable raps.
My mate Dews tried teaching me how to paint,
but I couldn't even hold the spray can.
When we'd horse around with a microphone
after drinking too many Heinekens,
I'd freeze up and forget what I wanted to spit.
Down in The Box, every Thursday night,
I heard MCs from Ōtara, Westmere,
Hendo and Avondale, drop lightning ciphers
over instrumentals by Primo, Swizz
Beats, and my favourite: Peanut Butter Wolf.
I thank those MCs for their gifts of attack.
Inside the coat check, the vending machine
coughed out Lucky Strikes for six bucks a pack.

STRAINS: ACAPULCO GOLD

Origin stories in the weed game are dubious.
If you research beneath the surface,
you will find they are often conflations—
marketing campaigns made to sell crosses.
Of this strain, every Dutch and Spanish
seedbank will claim to have the master cut.
Proto-coke smuggler Zachary Swan
rated it his all-time favourite smoke.
Arthur Lee wrote his best songs under its influence.
For two renegade poets named Ulises Lima
and Arturo Belano, it was bread and butter.
I had a line on it back in 2012: poeming
my way through a trance lasting six months.
It kept Bob Dylan in Acapulco, goin' on the run.

THE SECRET HISTORY OF NIKE AIR MAX

—for De Lo & Wiz

More tractive and durable than a pair of Bridgestones.
They were on the feet of a North Shore wild-styler
leaving his Krylon burners on panels and whole cars

across the after-dark lay-ups and trainyards of Aotearoa.
Long before they were picked up by Ponsonby's
monied yoga mothers pushing strollers to Dizengoff,

they were the kicks of choice for boutique shopgirls
who walked to work high straight from Calibre,
where the Breaks crew rolled heaters all night long.

Worn by rackers who slipped past snoozing Sunday morning
security guards working the door at Smith & Caughey's,
out into Queen Street with armloads of Polo and Nautica.

They were winged sandals for desperado drugstore cowboys
on some Matrix shit, filling their bags with boxes
of Actifeds under the feet of sumo-shaped pharmacists.

If you got pinched and ended up killing time in holding cells
or the Darwinian jungle of a prison remand yard,
the only way to keep hold of them was to use your fists.

DROPPED PIN: DEVONPORT, NORTH SHORE, AUCKLAND

Summer was a new pair of Birkenstocks.
Freud's *Totem and Taboo*
in a laminated
Dover edition, from Book Depository.

Swimming stoned
each night before sundown,
you floated at the edge of the Hauraki Gulf's
basin of tepid green water

somewhere between Takapuna and Rangitoto,
while blonde promo girls
in string bikinis posed beside rockpools
and children screamed

down the faces of small waves
on boogie-boards,
container ships reconfigured the horizon—
floating until you became the water,

floating until the water
became the memory of water
holding your body
again.

STRAINS: SLURRICANE

—for Blackmedal

Heart palpitations, sticky palms, globular sweat beads
scripting into paranoid lines along my forehead—
bro, that's only the start of what happened
when I first licked some cones of your Slurricane.
A Saturday night in February, late summer.
Berries and prunes in a bowl of Greek yoghurt
doused in gasoline is how it hit my nose
when I crushed a thumb-sized nug in the grinder.
Lovechild of Do-Si-Dos and the legendary Purple Punch:
when I put flame to the bong's glass slide cone
all those resin-caked, narcotic bracts and tiger-bright
pistils cindered into a creamy thick smoke,
coating my mouth and throat in burnt rubber terpenes.
The first was sweet; the second wrecked my shit.
Nothing unsettles like knowing a creeper's in the post.

*

If there's an afterlife there will certainly be a hell.
And in that hell, the devil will wear a balaclava
and roar up the San Fernando Valley
in a Chevrolet Blazer, and for all of eternity
yell out your shortcomings and weaknesses,
while you're stuck next to him in endless couchlock.
The bro Scotty Real from the *Dude Grows* show
would've called this state 'schoolboy stoned'.
I hadn't been that high since I was fifteen.
And when I crawled out of my writing shed
to lay down on the grass, to find my breath again,
the West Auckland police chopper hovered
in tightening concentric circles above the farm.
Game over: I was fucked. It all ends on a cop show.

My fenced outdoor compound of Exodus Cheese,
my tent of Banana Krumble late in flower—
I was a goner. Squad cars with wailing sirens
hoofed it along the ridge of Sunnyvale Road.
The chopper circled. They were closing in.
Just what I needed to be: an E-grade, middle-aged
poet with no money or job, up on cultivation charges.
And that's when I heard yelling at the gang house,
the idling of an eight-cylinder Commodore,
the breath-stopping claps of a Glock discharging.
Dogs barked. An agent of the Armed Offenders Squad
muffled orders at gangsters through a megaphone.
I've never been so relieved to live next to meth cooks.
Cops, outlaws. Around here they're putting in work.

THE GOLD PLAINS

—for Jeffrey Paparoa Holman

When I woke the gold plains were burning.
It was a still from an unmade Malik film.
Against the burnishing late-afternoon sun
dropping behind this reliquary outpost,
there was a weatherboard farmhouse
and oak tree struggling to keep their form.
I'm certain I saw a child playing there.
A mother with thin, languid arms
pegged sheets and towels to a clothesline.
Somewhere nearby would be the father,
sitting alone in his inherited silence
unable to name the emptiness inside him,
the same emptiness his father endured
before him and was unable to name.
Beneath me hummed the bus's driveshaft.
My thoughts returned to my own son.
When I looked back, the farmhouse was empty.
There was no mother hanging out washing,
no child at play. The gold plains burned.
I carried the father's silence away inside me.

DROPPED PIN: RAZORBACK ROAD, PŌKENO

It's a clear night. Hamish and Wiremu
crack stubbies of Waikato Draught.
Burn what's left from the outdoor season.
Words between them are slow in coming.
When they arrive, they are spare and pointed.
Tomorrow they will load rams on the Isuzu
into a holding pen made from old pallets,
for a man in Weymouth to fatten for Ramadan.
It's a clear night. Orion hurls his belt
and sword into a pool of creosote.
For Hamish, it will always be The Dipper.
The beer is warm. The weed makes them cough.
On the town side of the city border
gridded fields of diodes glow and hum.

INTERCITY BUS ELEGIES

INTERCITY BUS ELEGIES

When I left your yard to bus north again
strange portents gathered in the sky.

Westward the setting sun turned
clouds into curlicues of orange flame.

Tweakers and glue sniffers combed
the terminal for coins, cigarette butts.

Backpacking Mormon foot soldiers
with pressed shirts and bryl-slick haircuts

waited on rides out to the provinces.
I envied for a moment the rigour

of their faith; its unerring certitude.
Dusk was copper and rippled with static.

I wanted beyond my limits to believe.
Strange portents were hanging in the sky.

*

Summer taught the changing world's vernacular.
January brought us a Sunday afternoon

darkened at three by the inconsolable
drift of bushes burning across the Tasman.

Nightly the news reports chilled us.
We watched corporate drones in real time

murk Iran's top general near Baghdad.
An endgame seemed inevitable.

We found new words for hopeless.
February's humid lassitude

delivered death and car crashes.
We waited through summer's sleepless

soupy heat, keyed-in to panic,
for the empty stasis of tomorrow.

*

It was the hour of newspeak algorithms.
Our hectic world emptied, inverted.

Planes grounded behind closed borders.
The people wailed partisan folksongs

from their balcony prisons while coffins
heaped up in Bergamo and Madrid.

Rings of satellites orbiting the stratosphere
beamed back down granular images

of trenches furrowed behind mosques.
In Brooklyn's empty parking spaces

forklifts filled makeshift mortuaries.
Without marker the dead put to their rest

became black pixels, memorial smudges.
Night after night the news reports chilled us.

*

Past Norton Road's jaundiced factories,
corroding foundries and scrapyards

walks a man with outstretched arms.
His palms are facing upwards,

aiming a supplication at heaven.
God updates his image for the times.

He will come to us in teal scrubs,
rubber sneakers and a surgical mask

carolling his ventilator gospels
from a kingdom of disinfectant clouds.

Traffic stalls to brake-light haze.
Drivers download the day's ending.

A stray dog shits beneath a lamppost.
The path the man walks on is a motorway.

*

From the new truck stop near Taupiri
late capitalism's gleaming coronas

downsize the night's first stars.
Backdraught from passing freighters

shakes the bus cab and chassis.
In every seat: an islanded traveller's

myopic face made lunar by screen glow.
Next to me a woman from Holland

swiping through her Kindle novel
mutters about the gone world.

Mallards crest an arc over the urupā.
Seaward the dark river slithers—

eerily, unmediated and succinctly,
light sliding off its black liquid scales.

*

On every bus there rides a lay evangelist.
Tonight's tweaker preacher clambers

along the aisle clutching at seats,
laying down his vision of original sin.

Pupils sprung from firing points of meth
he yammers louder than a rock drill

spitting parables at anyone who'll listen—
'Does hate have a home in your heart?'

He spooks a couple of young backpackers—
'If it does, the Devil's got your papers.'

The driver yells at him to sit back down.
He goes on raving in the darkness—

'My god has no name other than God.
The Devil's got papers on every one of us.'

*

Above the racetrack at Hampton Downs
the sky discharges like a giant capacitor.

Forked lightning letters the space in between
with a jump cut of twenty-five years

back to night school, at Manukau Polytechnic.
We're dropouts, baby dopers and drinkers.

The tutor, a former navy drill sergeant,
blasts us again with variants of Ohm's Law.

I'm wedged between them in the front row:
the boy whose heart will blow out on speed,

the boy whose life will end as a flashpoint
between the terminals of an 11kV transformer—

ignorant and blazed while the tutor barks on
about fault currents finding the short path to earth.

ACKNOWLEDGEMENTS

Some of these poems first appeared in *Mayhem, Poetry New Zealand Yearbook* (2021 and 2022), *Stasis, takahē, The Spinoff Friday Poem* and *The New Zealand Poet Laureate blog.*

For their aroha and solidarity during the writing of this book I am thankful to Jeffrey Paparoa Holman, Victor Billot, Martin Edmond, Tracey Slaughter, Richard Reeve, Peter Madden, Dave Wright, August and Amy and the whole Tonkin/Howe/Mignault whānau.

Thanks to David Eggleton, to editor Lynley Edmeades, Sue Wootton, Imogen Coxhead and Fiona Moffat at Otago University Press.

Thanks are due also to Steve Braunias, Newsroom and the Surrey Hotel for generously providing a few nights' stay in a room with a balcony where I had the time and space to tinker on an early draft of this collection.

And lastly, Schaeffer Lemalu, who first read a cohesive draft of this collection and whose insightful comments helped give it form. This one's for you, bro.

These poems might not have been written without the groundbreaking genetic work of Dave Watson, Ed Rosenthal, Nevil Schoenmakers and Scott Blakey, Subcool and Franco Loja. Bless up.

Published by Otago University Press
533 Castle Street
Dunedin, New Zealand
university.press@otago.ac.nz
www.otago.ac.nz/press

First published 2022
ISBN 978-1-99-004834-0

Published with the assistance of Creative New Zealand

Editor: Lynley Edmeades
Cover artwork by Peter Madden

Printed in New Zealand by Ligare.